D0178850

*art*file

Creatures

*Ready-to-use,
copyright-free art & graphics
for the busy, budget-wise
designer.*

Φ

PHAIDON • OXFORD

Published by
Phaidon Press Limited
Musterlin House
Jordan Hill Road
Oxford
England
OX2 8DP

First published 1990

© **Graphic Books International Ltd.**
P.O. Box 349
Newlands Building
Lowlands
Guernsey
Channel Islands (UK)

A CIP catalogue record for this
book is available from the
British Library

ISBN 0 7148 2665 0

Printed in Great Britain by
Penshurst Press Ltd.
Tunbridge Wells, Kent

The art of using **art**file

This book is just one in a series of Artfiles, each of which provides hundreds of ready-to-use images designed to add an instant professional touch to print, publicity and all forms of graphic communication at a fraction of the cost of original art.

All of the images contained in this book are yours to use in almost any way you wish. No reproduction fees are required and the copyright will not be infringed, provided that the Artfile images are not incorporated into any form of product or service that could be considered by the publishers or copyright-holder as an alternative or competitive art source.

When using Artfile images as part of a design service for fee-paying clients, it is advisable that clients are made fully aware that the designs in part or whole are not unique, exclusive or their copyright.

Creating original illustrations and graphics has always been time-consuming and expensive, but with Artfile you have hundreds of images at your fingertips for less than the cost of one single piece of original art.

With Artfile, even the inexperienced non-designer can quickly and easily transform newsletters,advertisements, leaflets, etc. into effective commnications. Experienced designers will appreciate the numerous ways in which each illustration can be reproduced and modified but for those who have limited creative skills and knowledge of reproduction techniques, we offer the following advice and a selection of demonstration layouts.

Firstly, take time to familiarise yourself with the contents of each book. This will help you to create ideas that spring from material that you have available rather than trying to find images to meet pre- conceived ideas. The miniature visual index provided with each volume will help you to find illustrations in just a few seconds. If you purchase several Artfile volumes, we would suggest either that copies are made of the index pages or that they are removed to create a master index.

How you use your Artfile art will depend on your personal working methods. The majority of users may wish to separate the art sheets and place them in a ring binder or filing system. Breaking down the book into individual sheets will make reproducing the art easier and will be essential if you wish to scan-in images for Desktop Publishing.

If required, Artfile images can be cut out and pasted directly into position on your designs but often you will need to make an enlarged or reduced copy of the illustration. With strong, simple designs a quality photocopy may be sufficient, but the best results will be obtained by making photo-mechanical prints using a reprographic camera to create copies for use in artwork.

It should be noted that all images in Artfile are 'line' images, even when they may appear to be photographs. The special effect screen and tints that have been used are coarse and can therefore be treated as 'dot for dot' line copy by your printer. The majority of images can be enlarged significantly, but may need a little retouching on extreme enlargements. Most of the images will reduce satisfactorily down to even 20% of original size, but careful exposure will be necessary to avoid loss of detail. Our miniature visual index is a good guide as to what you can expect when images are reduced down to 20%. The recommended reduction for photo-based images and designs with tints or fine shading is 50% if they are being reproduced by standard litho printing

If you wish to use Artfile images for use on Desktop Publishing systems, we would suggest that the best results will be obtained by using only the simpler, bolder line images. Fine detail and screened images will be difficult to scan satisfactorily. Selected images from Artfile will soon become available on a computer disc: look out for announcements from the publishers.

As can be seen in the sample layouts, each Artfile illustration can be reproduced in several forms. Images can be enlarged and cropped, flipped from left to right, reproduced as a negative, tinted and coloured and of course combined with many other design components, including type and borders. With a little creative imagination, Artfile art components can transform basic advertisements, posters, leaflets etc. into attention-demanding layouts.

To expand your design skills and to obtain a fuller understanding of the reproduction process we would recommend that you invest in one or more books on layout and artwork techniques, usually available from major bookstores and art supplies shops, where you will also discover many other useful materials and design aids.

Artfile provides you with quality illustration and design components. Turning them into effective designs that reflect your creative imagination and your clients' communications objectives is your task - but Artfile can make it a great deal easier, faster and more economical.

All great designers have had to learn to develop their skills, you too through observation and experimentation will improve your creative work by taking Artfile images and transforming them into designs that get results that more than justify every investment you make in the Artfile library of art source books.

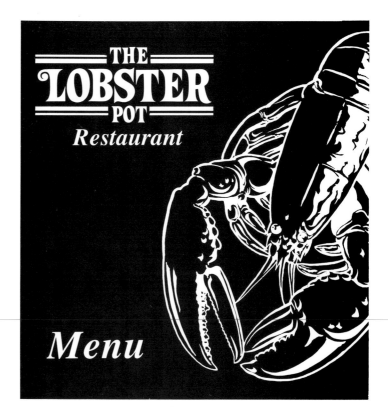

Visual
Index

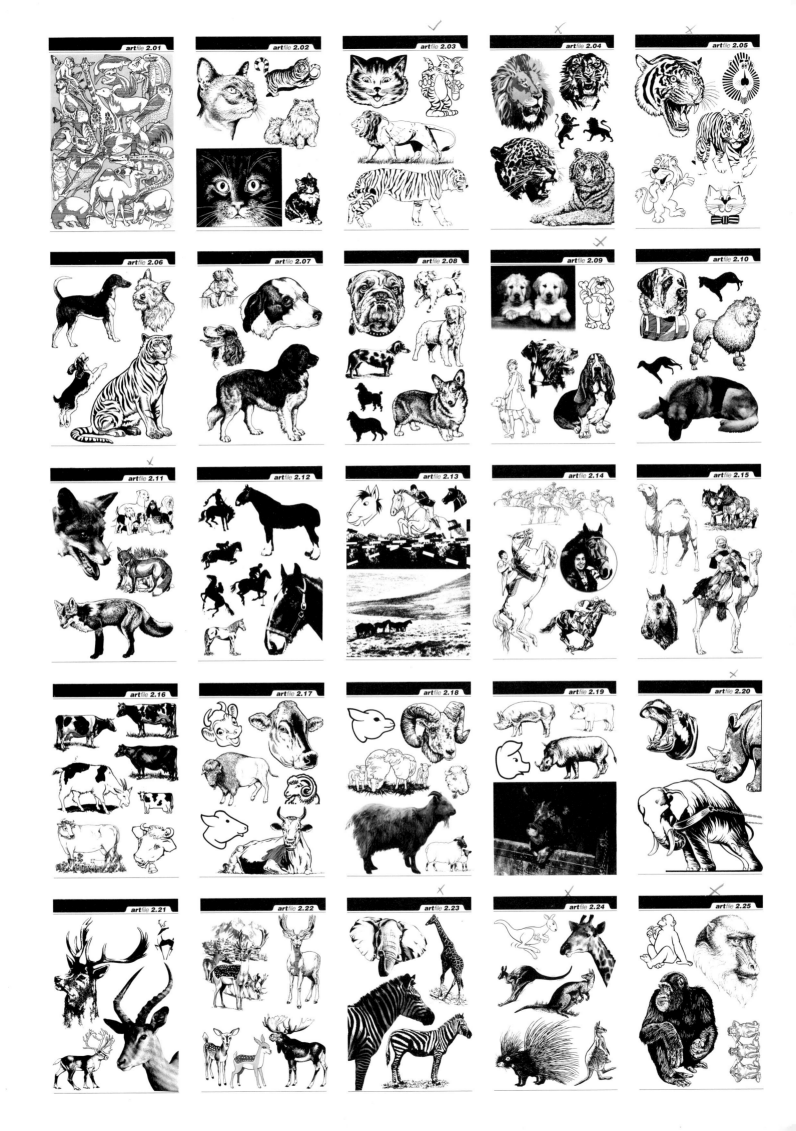

artfile 2.26
artfile 2.27
artfile 2.28
artfile 2.29
artfile 2.30
artfile 2.31
artfile 2.32
artfile 2.33
artfile 2.34
artfile 2.35
artfile 2.36
artfile 2.37
artfile 2.38
artfile 2.39
artfile 2.40
artfile 2.41
artfile 2.42
artfile 2.43
artfile 2.44
artfile 2.45
artfile 2.46
artfile 2.47
artfile 2.48
artfile 2.49
artfile 2.50

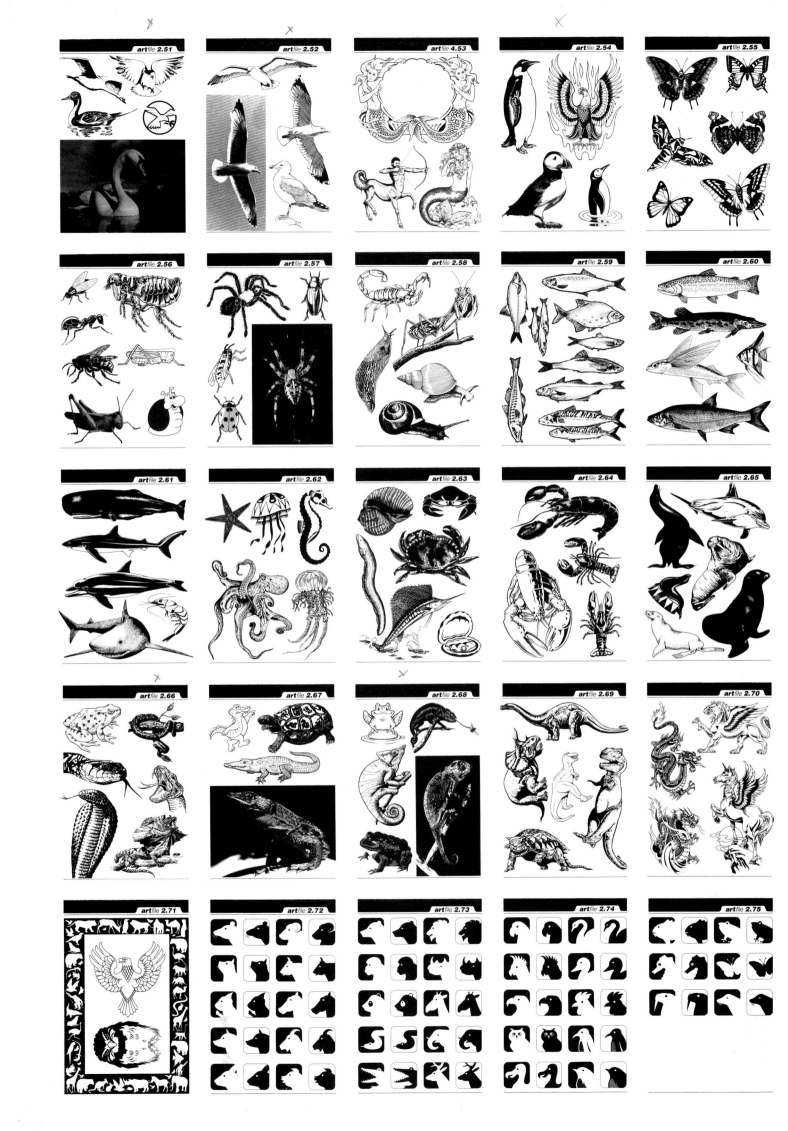

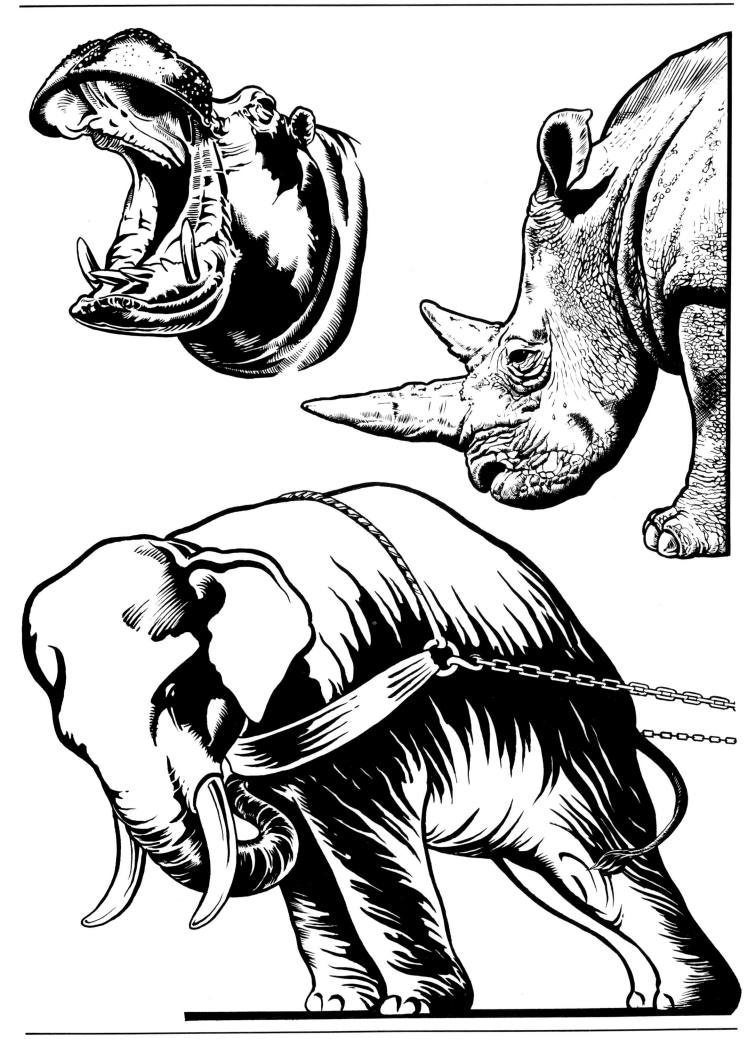

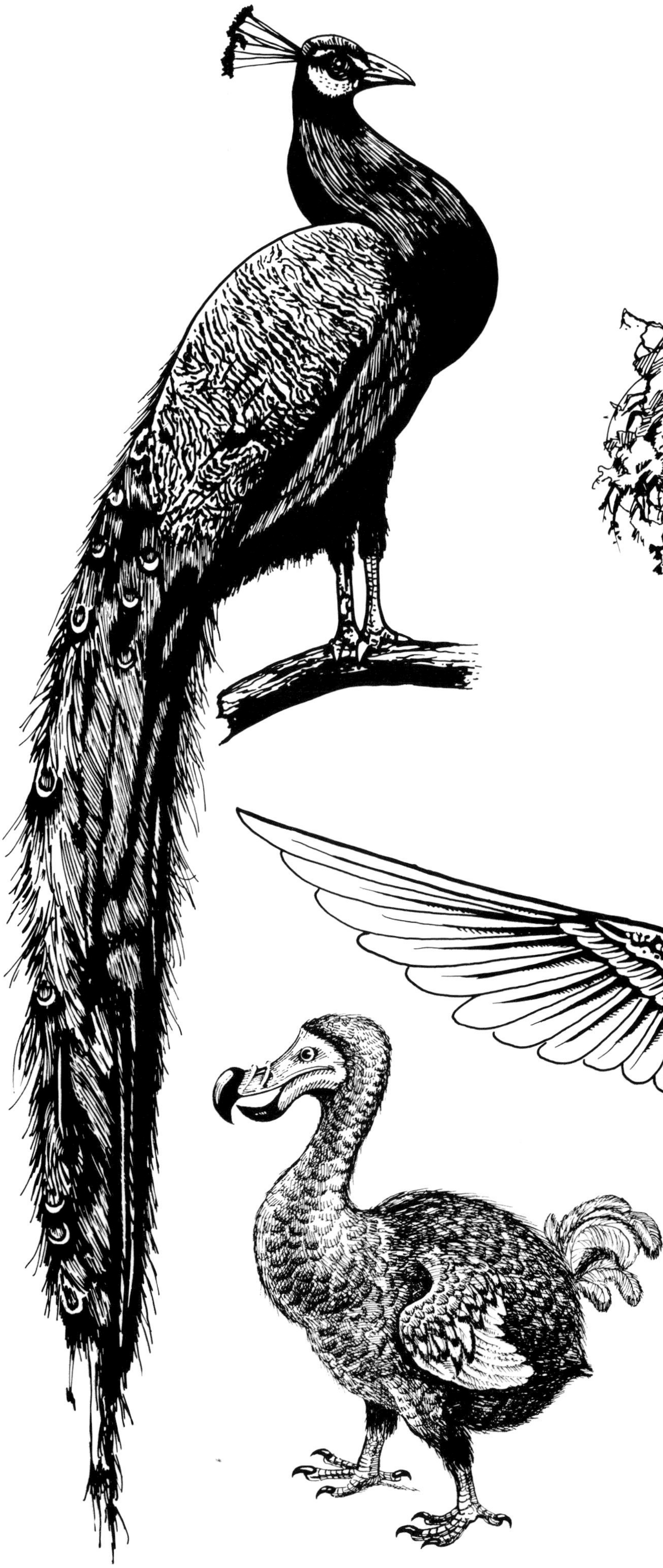

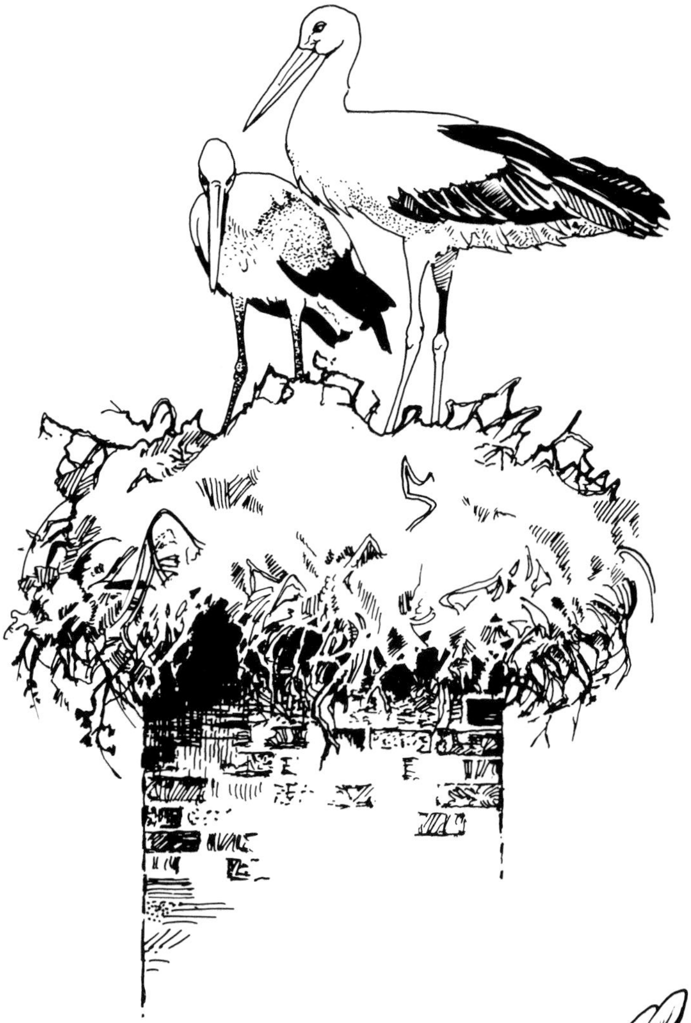

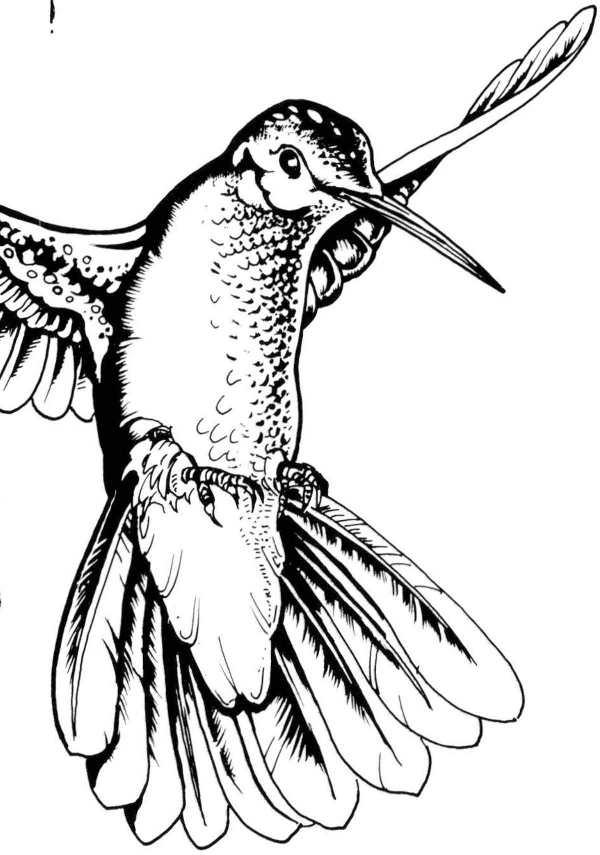

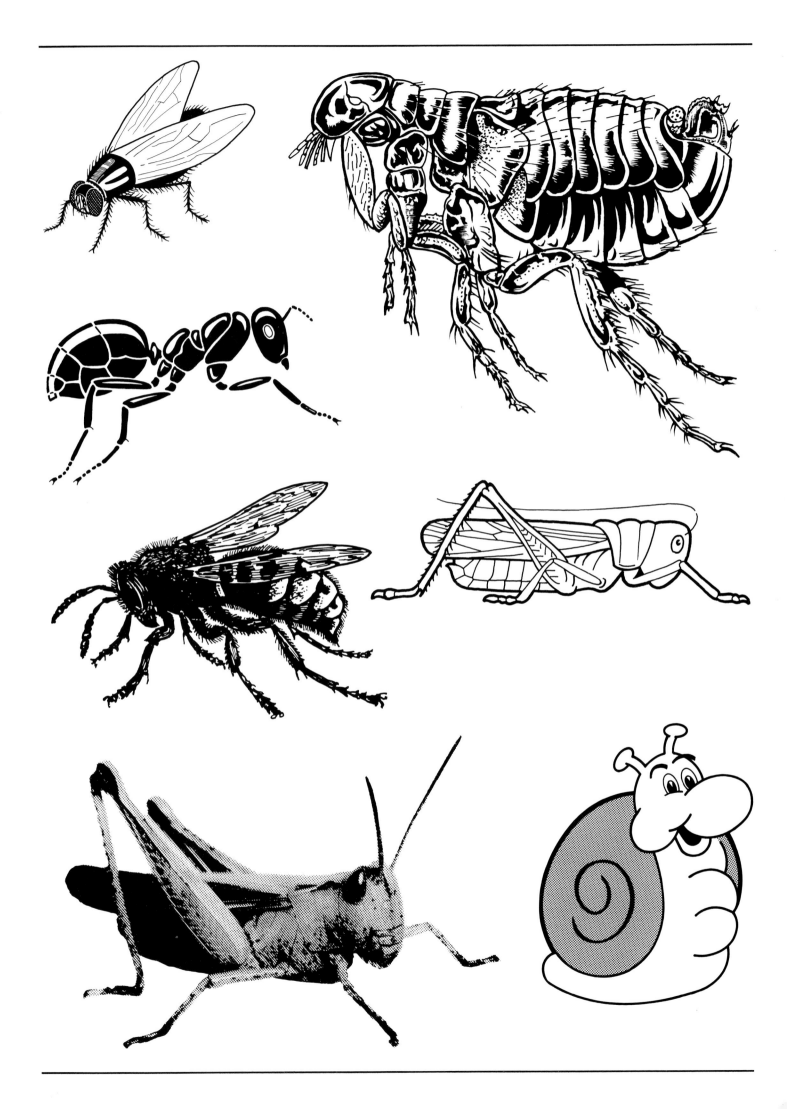

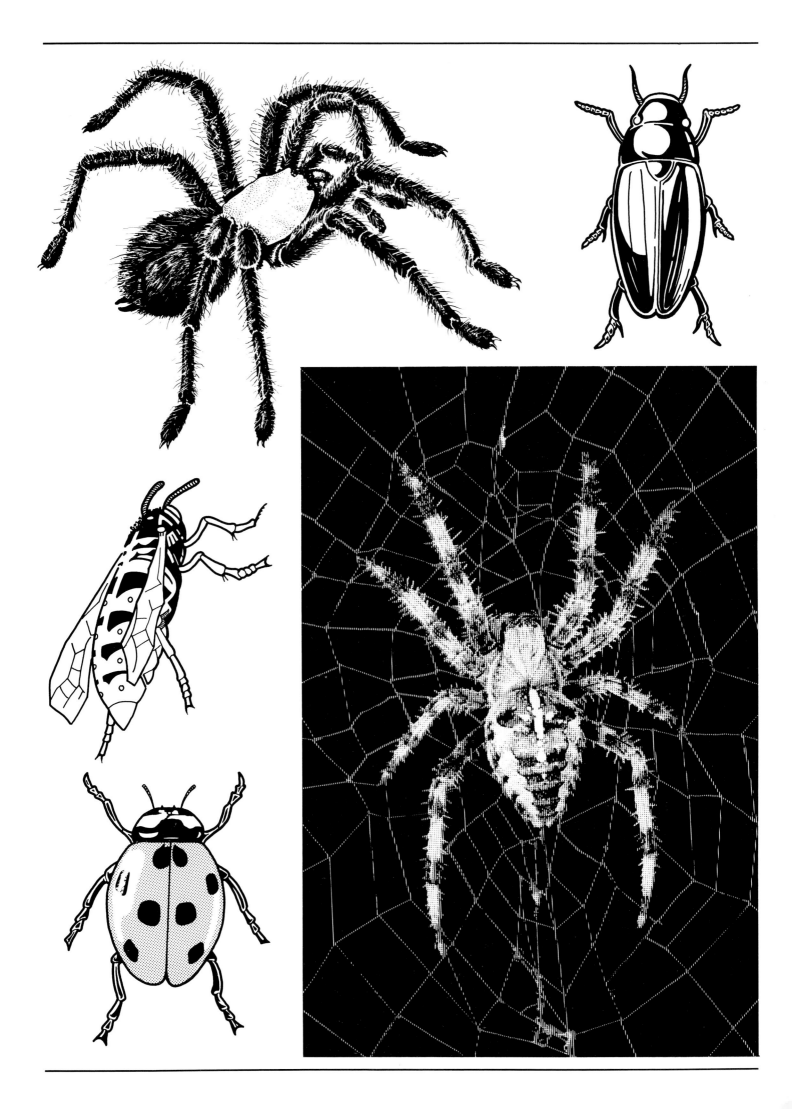

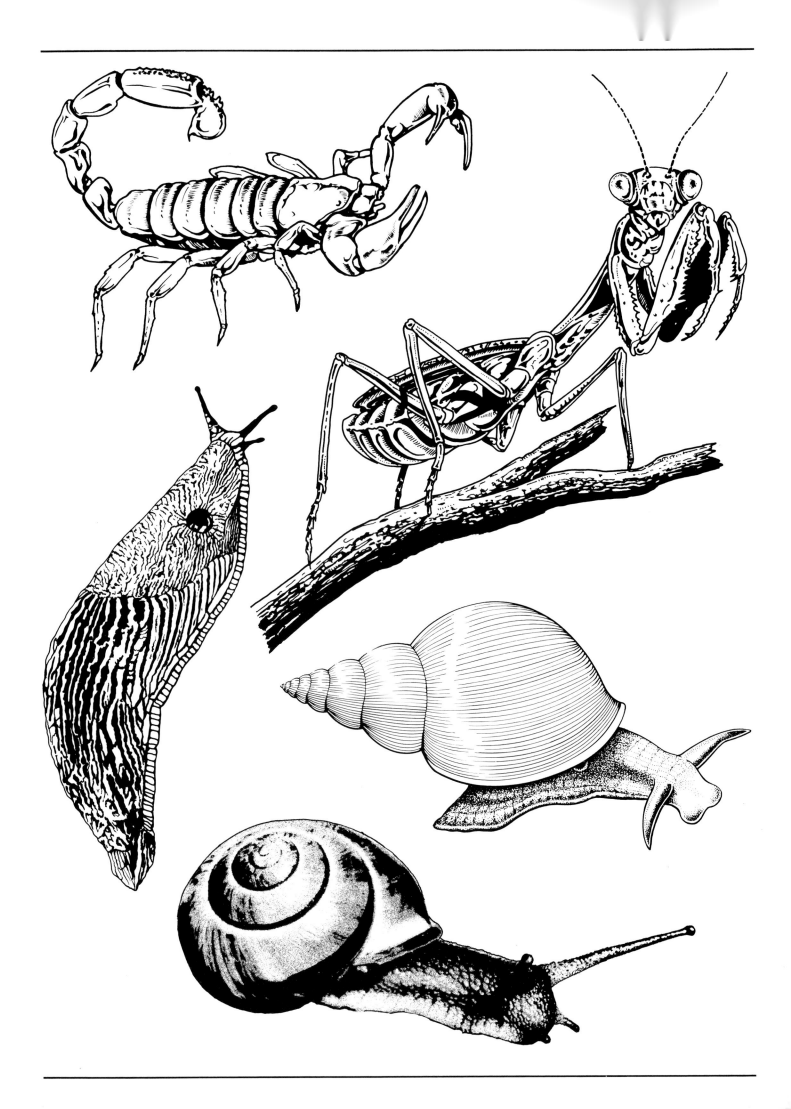

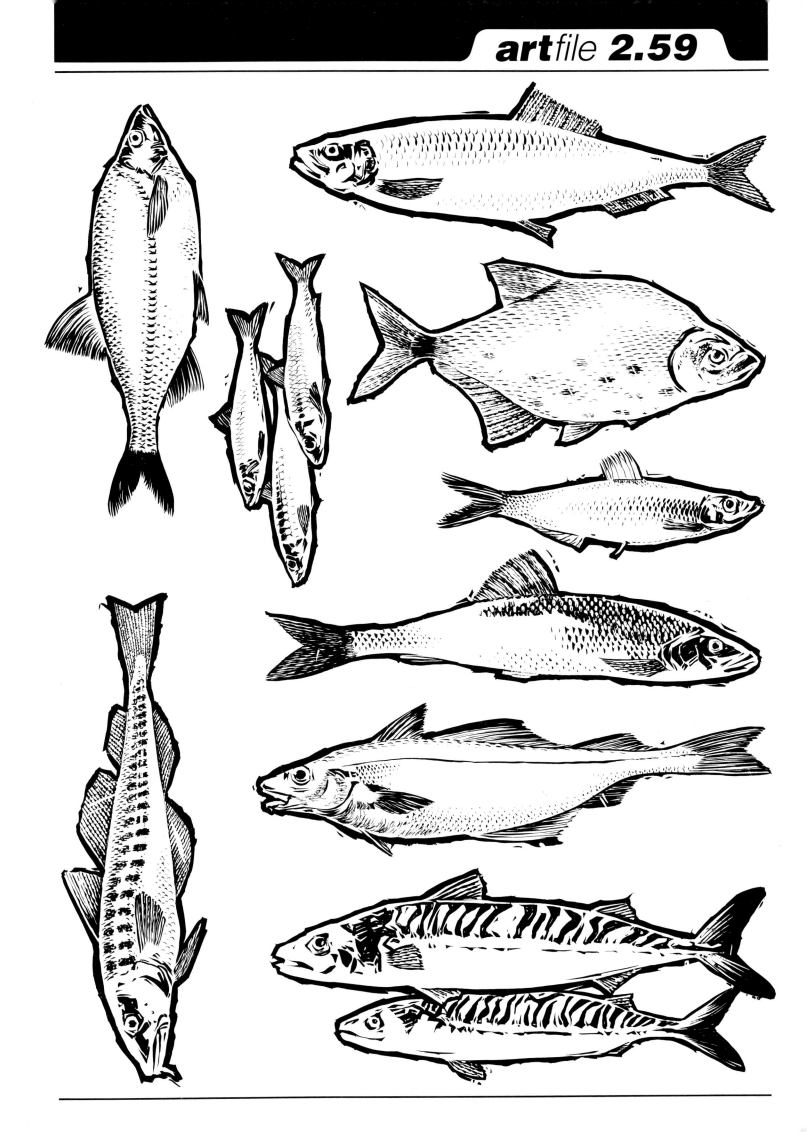

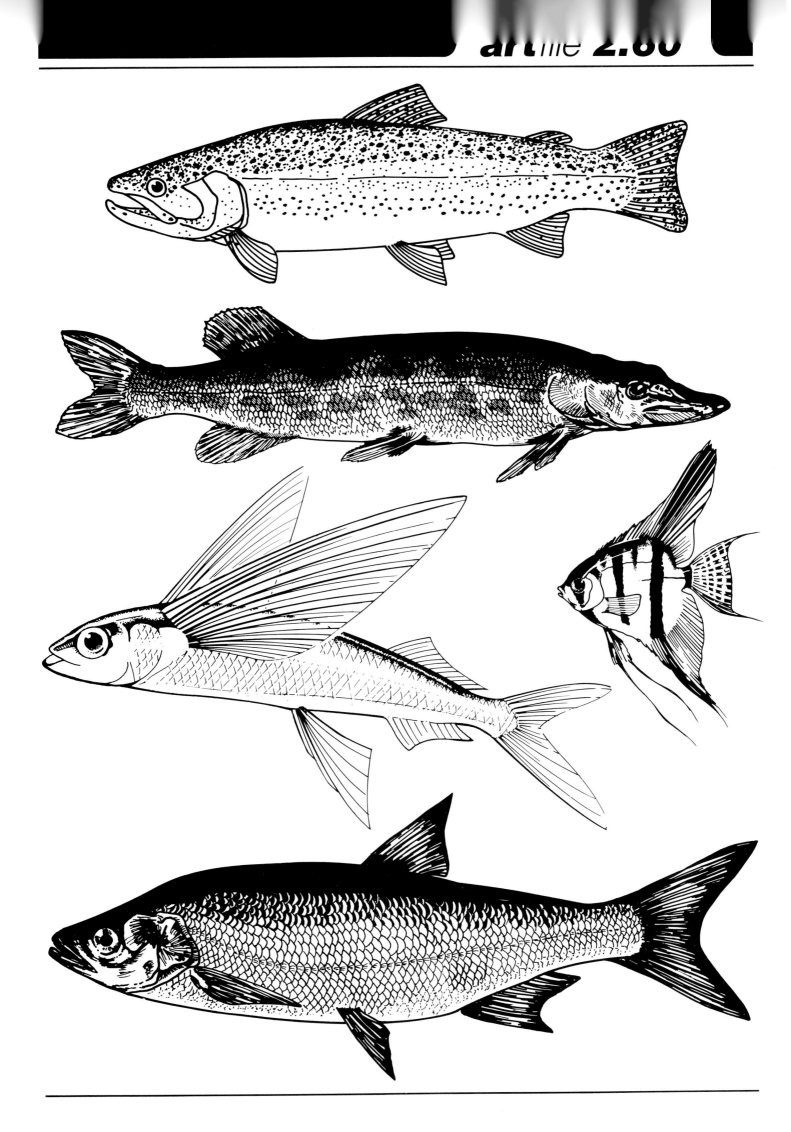

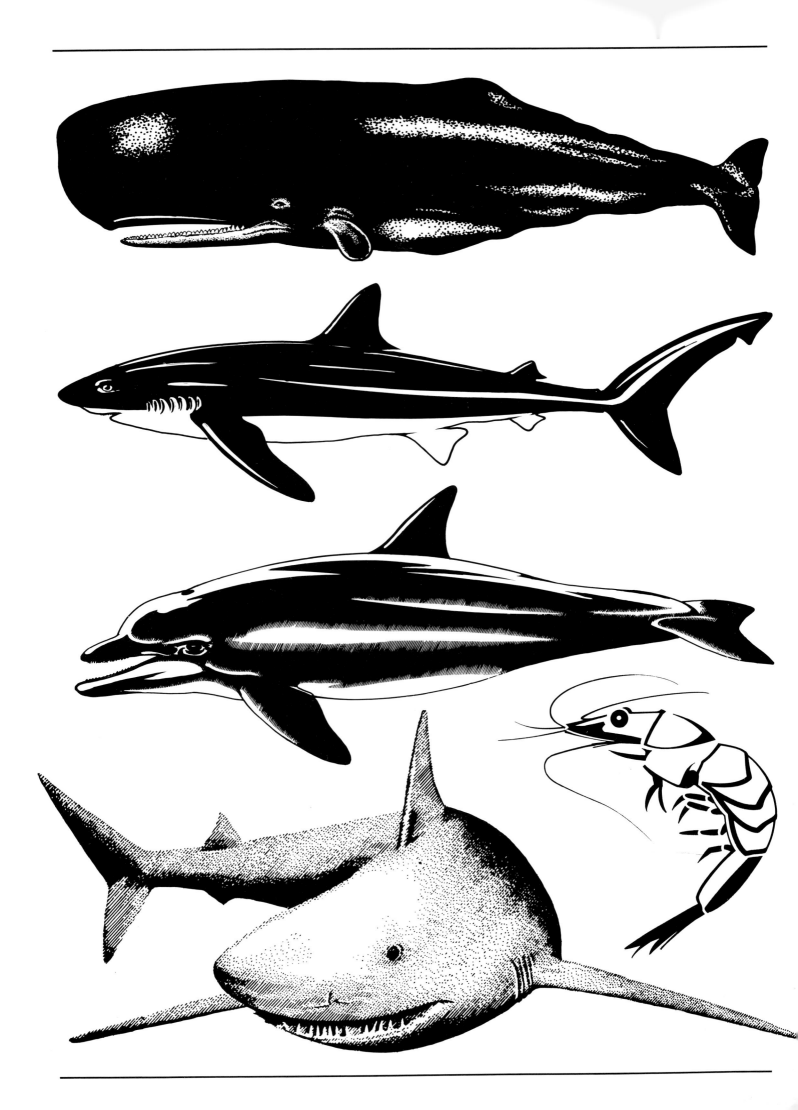

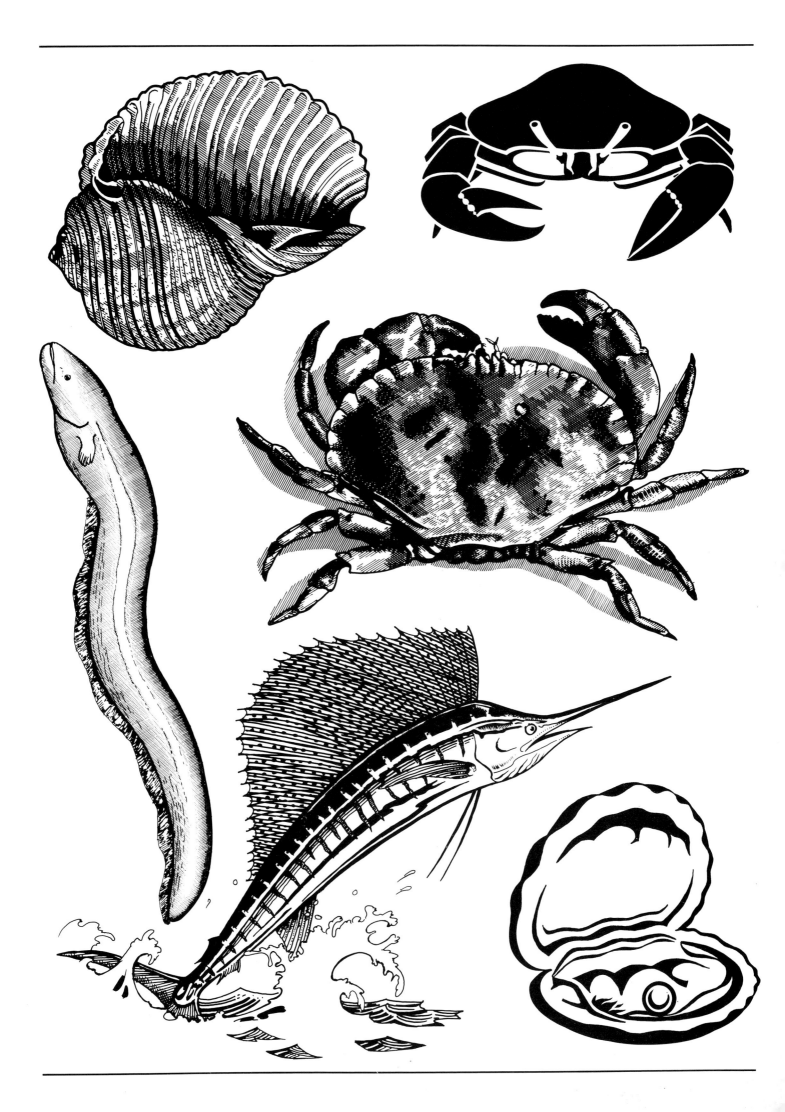

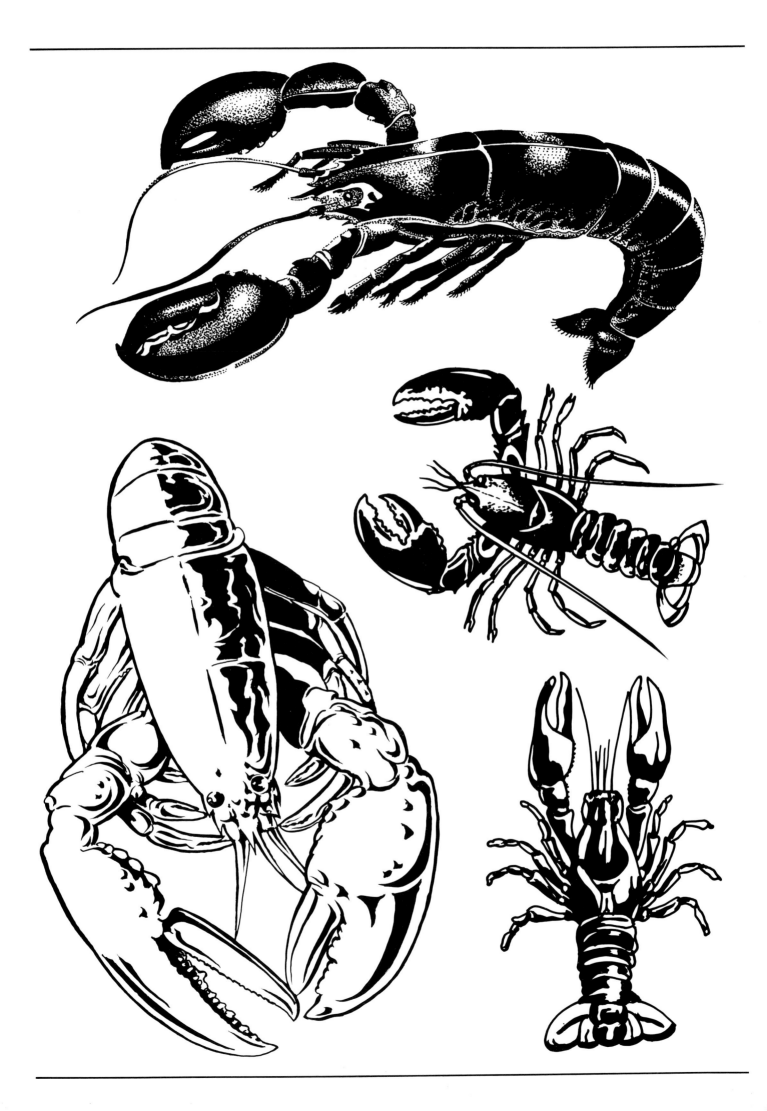

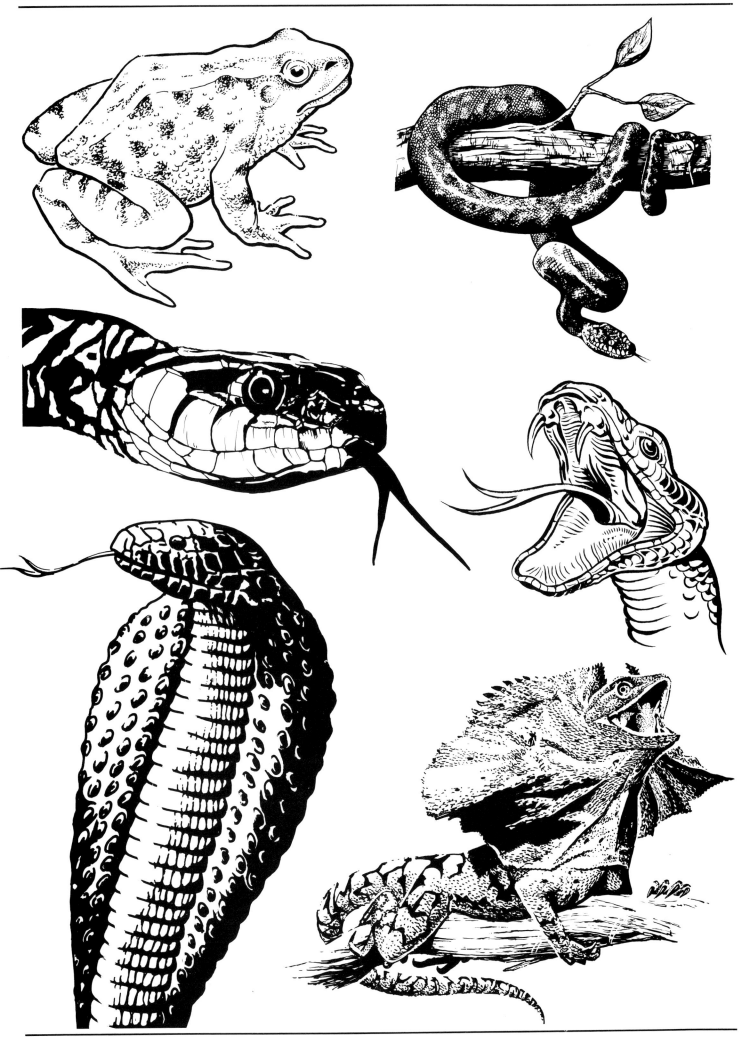

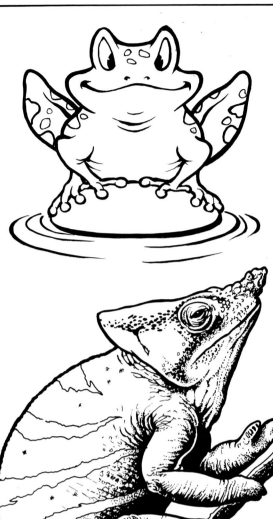

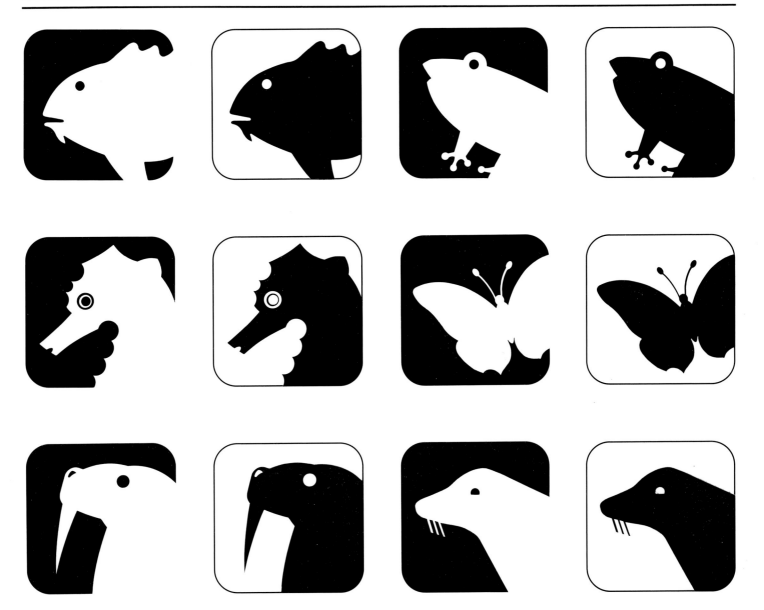